Chief Joseph Surrenders

Written by Douglas M. Rife

Illustrated by Bron Smith

Teaching & Learning Company

1204 Buchanan St., P.O. Box 10
Carthage, IL 62321-0010

This book belongs to

_____

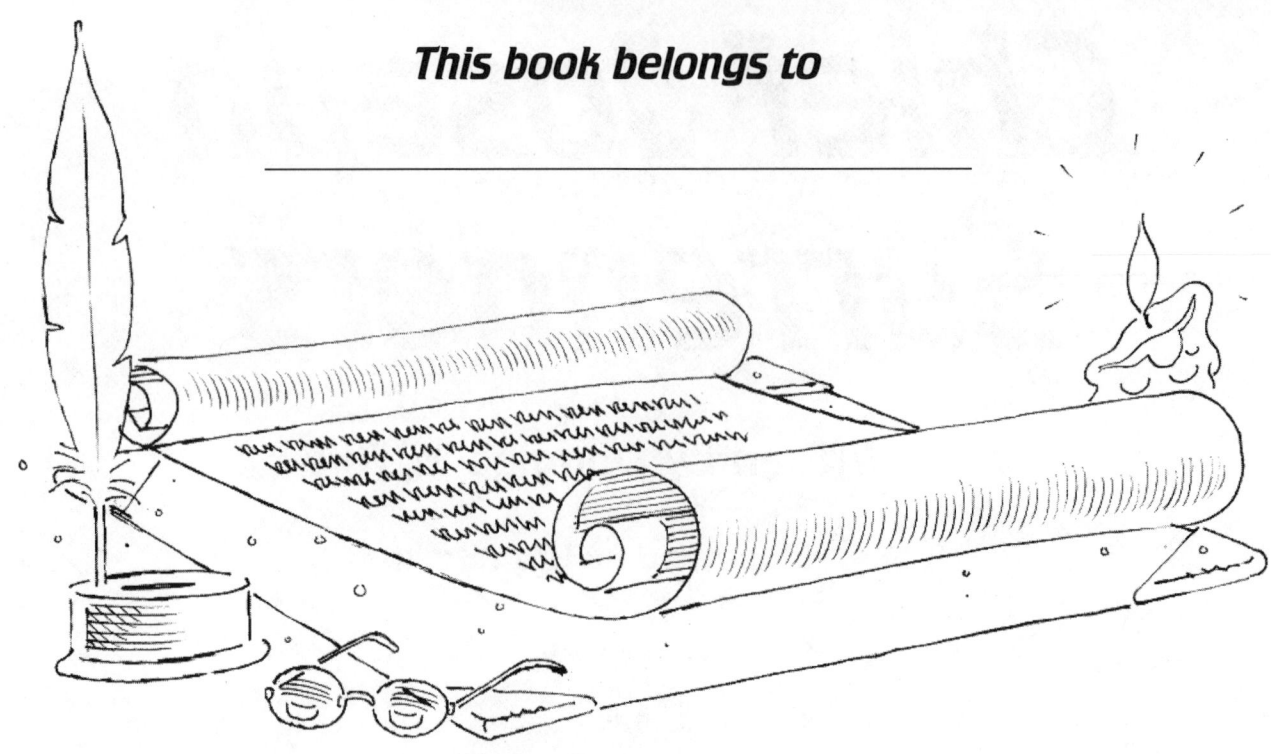

I would like to thank Terri Torretto and Dover Publications
for their quick responses to my permission requests.

Cover drawing by Mark Mason

Copyright © 2002, Teaching & Learning Company

ISBN No. 1-57310-348-9

Printing No. 987654321

Teaching & Learning Company
1204 Buchanan St., P.O. Box 10
Carthage, IL 62321-0010

The purchase of this book entitles teachers to make copies for use in their individual classrooms only. This book, or any part of it, may not be reproduced in any form for any other purposes without prior written permission from the Teaching & Learning Company. It is strictly prohibited to reproduce any part of this book for an entire school or school district, or for commercial resale. The above permission is exclusive of the cover art, which may not be reproduced.

All rights reserved. Printed in the United States of America.

Table of Contents

Objectives 5

North American Tribes Map **Handout 1** . . . 6

Time Line **Handout 2** 7

Time Line Activity **Handout 3** 17

Time Line Questions **Handout 4** 18

Who's Who? Matching **Handout 5** 19

Map Test **Handout 6** 20

Chief Joseph's Surrender Speech
   To the Teacher 21

Chief Joseph's Surrender Speech
   at Bear Paw Battle **Handout 7** 22

Chief Joseph's Surrender Speech at Bear Paw
   Battle Review **Handout 8** 23

Editorial Writing **To the Teacher** 24

San Francisco Chronicle **Handout 9** 26

Matching **Handout 10** 29

New York Times **Handout 11** 30

New York Times Review **Handout 12** 34

Editorial Cartoons **To the Teacher** 35

"Every Dog . . ." Editorial
   Cartoon **Handout 13** 39

"Every Dog . . ." Editorial
   Cartoon Questions **Handout 14** 40

"Move On!" Editorial
   Cartoon **Handout 15** 41

"Move On!" Editorial
   Cartoon Questions **Handout 16** 42

Bibliography 43

Answer Key 45

Dear Teacher or Parent,

The events that took place in the summer and fall of 1877 to the Nez Percé were tragic. The events that year also mirrored what had happened since the first Europeans landed in North America. From the very beginning, the clash between the two cultures was evident. The European concept of land ownership was totally foreign to the Native Americans who believed no one person could own the land. They believed it was owned in common. At first, the Native Americans believed that they could live in harmony with the Europeans but that quickly changed. And once the Europeans had a foothold in the New World, they just kept coming. Soon they began moving west. The Europeans' hunger for land soon crowded out the Native Americans. The farther west the Europeans moved the more conflict there was between the two groups. This scenario was played out over and over until the entire North American continent was under European control.

The Nez Percé, an Indian tribe whose ancestral home had been in the Wallowa Valley for thousands of years, were forced from their homelands through a series of treaties with the United States government. When Chief Joseph and his band of Nez Percé, referred to as the non-treaty Indians, said they would not leave, the government came to remove them. A chase ensued and 800 or so of the Nez Percé were pursued nearly to Canada before they surrendered. The tiny band of warriors and their families were wounded, cold and starving when they surrendered on October 5th. The surrender from Chief Joseph was a heartfelt and plaintive speech, one of the most eloquent speeches in American history.

The purpose of this book is to provide a brief history of the Nez Percé and the war that took place in 1877, as well as a better understanding of Chief Joseph's surrender speech through activities that help students focus on its meaning and impact. The book introduces the students to the Nez Percé through a series of activities related to the Nez Percé time line handout at the beginning of the book.

Also included in the book is an editorial from the *New York Times*. The essay deplores the injustice of the war with the Nez Percé and defends their right to live on their ancestral lands. The students will examine editorial writing and be asked to write an editorial of their own. The book also includes two editorial cartoons that first appeared in *Harper's Weekly* drawn by Thomas Nast, the most well-known American editorial cartoonist of the 19th century.

Sincerely,

Douglas

Douglas M. Rife

Objectives

After completing the following activities	the students should be able to . . .
Time Line	1. identify North American Native American tribes 2. identify the Nez Percé ancestral homelands 3. understand the sequence of events that led up to the Nez Percé War in 1877 4. draw conclusions about the reasons for the war
Chief Joseph's Surrender Speech	1. understand the significance of the speech 2. identify the reasons for the Nez Percé surrender 3. analyze the speech for facts, references and meaning
Editorial Writing	1. recognize the difference between opinion and fact in newspaper writing 2. compare two news stories 3. identify fact, bias and opinion 4. judge the opinion of an editorial 5. write one's own editorial
Editorial Cartoons	1. identify caricature 2. identify symbolism 3. draw conclusions about the meaning in a cartoon or print 4. identify differing opinions 5. identify stereotyping 6. identify racism 7. draw own editorial cartoons 8. judge a cartoonist's viewpoint

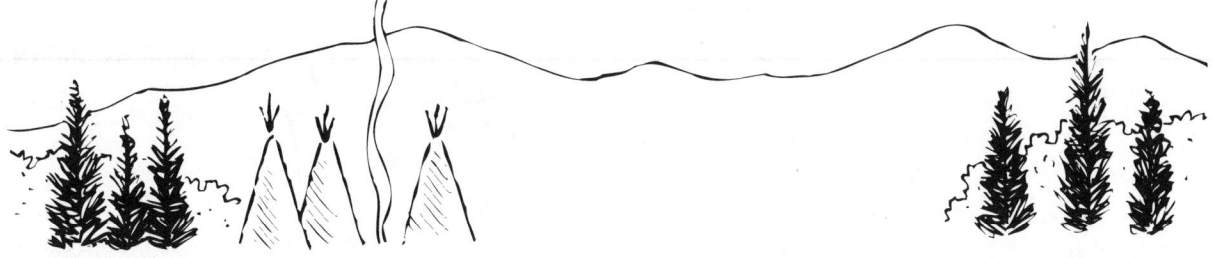

North American Tribes

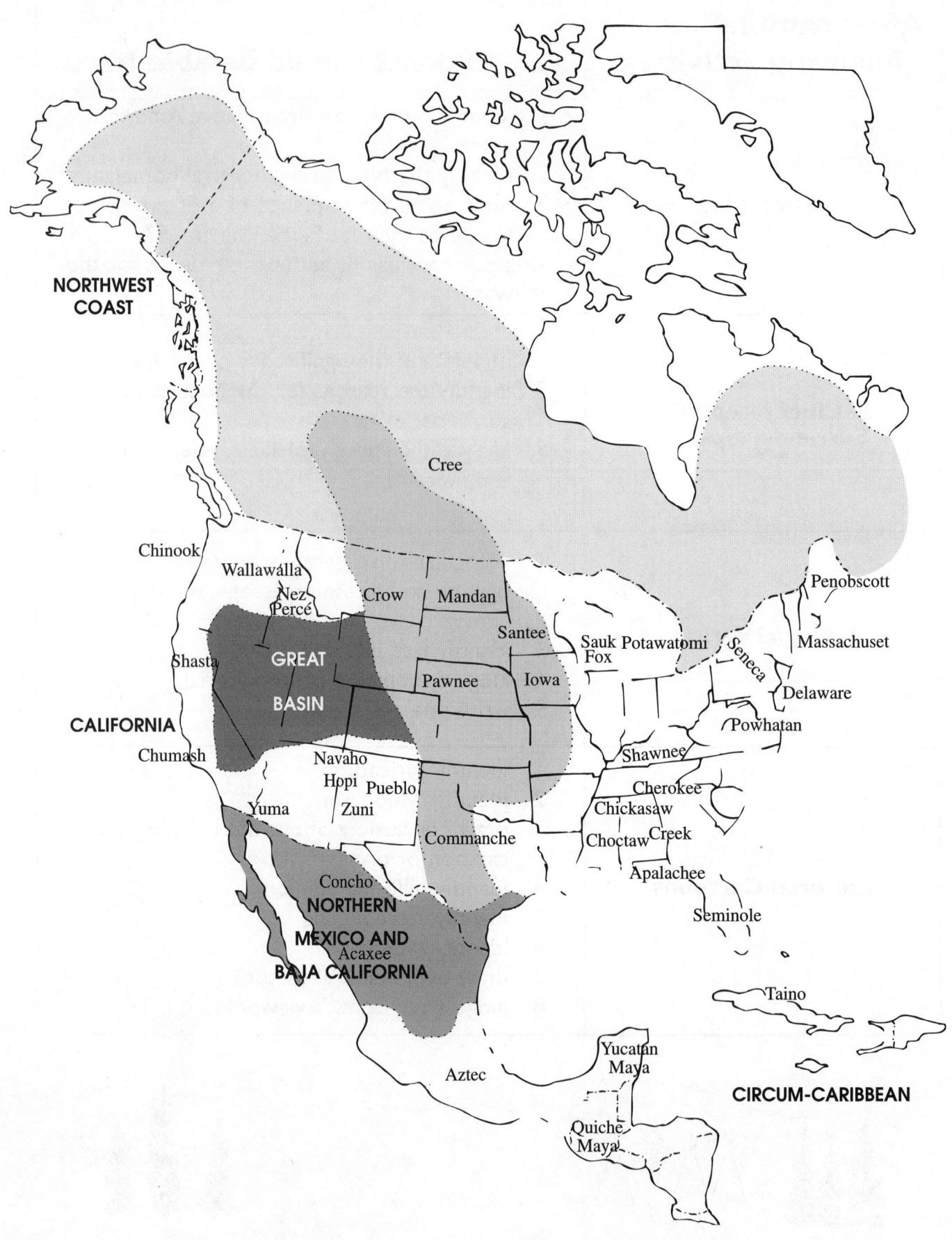

Handout 1

Time Line

1786 Tuekakas is born (later known as Chief Joseph).

1805 Meriwether Lewis and William Clark meet the Nez Percé while on their famous expedition from St. Louis, Missouri to the Pacific Ocean. (The term *Nez Percé* is a corrupted version of the term *pierced nose*. Some Native American tribes did pierce their noses, though this was not common among the Nez Percé.) Lewis and Clark were sent on the expedition by President Thomas Jefferson to explore the continent and report back to him. The Nez Percé feed the men in the expedition. Lewis and Clark think highly of the Nez Percé, who they refer to as the Chopunnish. The Nez Percé call themselves the *Nee-Me-Poo*, which means "the people." Archaeological evidence indicates that the Nee-Me-Poo have lived in the Wallowa Valley for possibly 13,000 years.

1836 The first Christian church is established in the Wallowa Valley at Lapwai, Idaho, by Presbyterian minister, Reverend Henry Spalding and his wife Eliza.

1838 Tu-eka-kas is given the name Joseph.

1839 Old Chief Joseph, Tu-eka-kas, is baptized by Reverend Henry Spalding.

Handout 2

Time Line

1840 Hin-mah-too-yah-lat-kekht or Thunder Rolling Down from the Mountains (Young Chief Joseph) is born in the Land of Winding Waters, which we now call the Wallowa Valley. This boy later became known by non-Native Americans as Young Chief Joseph. Young Chief Joseph was born to a quiet chief of the Nez Percé Indians, whose ancestors had lived in that valley for thousands of years. There the tribe had lived, hunting, farming and raising their children for centuries before. Young Chief Joseph's father was Tuekakas. His father later became known as Chief Joseph. Chief Joseph was married to Khapkhaponimi, which means "loose bark on a tree." Chief Joseph and Khapkhaponimi had five children. They had two daughters—Celia and Elawinonmi. They also had three sons—Young Chief Joseph, Shugan which means "brown" and Ollokot, which means "frog."

Time Line

Oregon Trail

Oregon Trail

Thousands of Americans traveled west following the Oregon Trail, which took them directly past the ancestral lands of the Nez Percé.

Handout 2

Time Line

1847 Over 4000 new settlers come to Oregon along the Oregon Trail. The white settlers bring a measles epidemic with them that kills over half of the Cayuse Indians. Murders by the Cayuse Indians at the Marcus Whitman Mission cause trouble between the Nez Percé and the white settlers.

1842 Traditionally the Nez Percé did not have one great chief, but many chiefs who led small bands of Nez Percé within the larger group. In an effort to make it easier for the United States to negotiate with the Nez Percé Indian subagent, Dr. Elijah White, coerces the Nez Percé to accept Ellis, an English-speaking Nez Percé chief, as chief of all of the Nez Percé. Because Ellis could speak English, White argued, it would be easier to talk to and negotiate with the Nez Percé.

1855 The first treaty between the United States government and the Nez Percé grants the Wallowa Valley to the Nez Percé. The treaty recognizes the Wallowa Valley as the Nez Percé homeland. This treaty was signed by Old Chief Joseph and some 57 other chiefs and negotiated by Isaac I. Steven, Governor and Superintendent of Indian Affairs. The treaty was ratified in 1859.

Handout 2

Time Line

1860 Gold is discovered on the Nez Percé lands, mining begins almost immediately in violation of the 1855 treaty.

1863 A second treaty is negotiated. During the negotiations, however, when Old Chief Joseph realizes that the United States government is trying to reduce the Nez Percé lands, Old Chief Joseph abandons the talks. A treaty is signed by Chief Lawyer.

1871 Tuekakas (Old Chief Joseph) dies and his son, Joseph, becomes the leader of the Wallowa band of non-treaty Nez Percé.

1873 President Ulysses Grant signs an executive order to stop settlement in a newly created Wallowa Reservation for the Nez Percé.

1875 President Grant signs an order revoking his earlier order, opening up the Wallowa Valley for settlement. Young Chief Joseph and the non-treaty Nez Percé decide not to go to war.

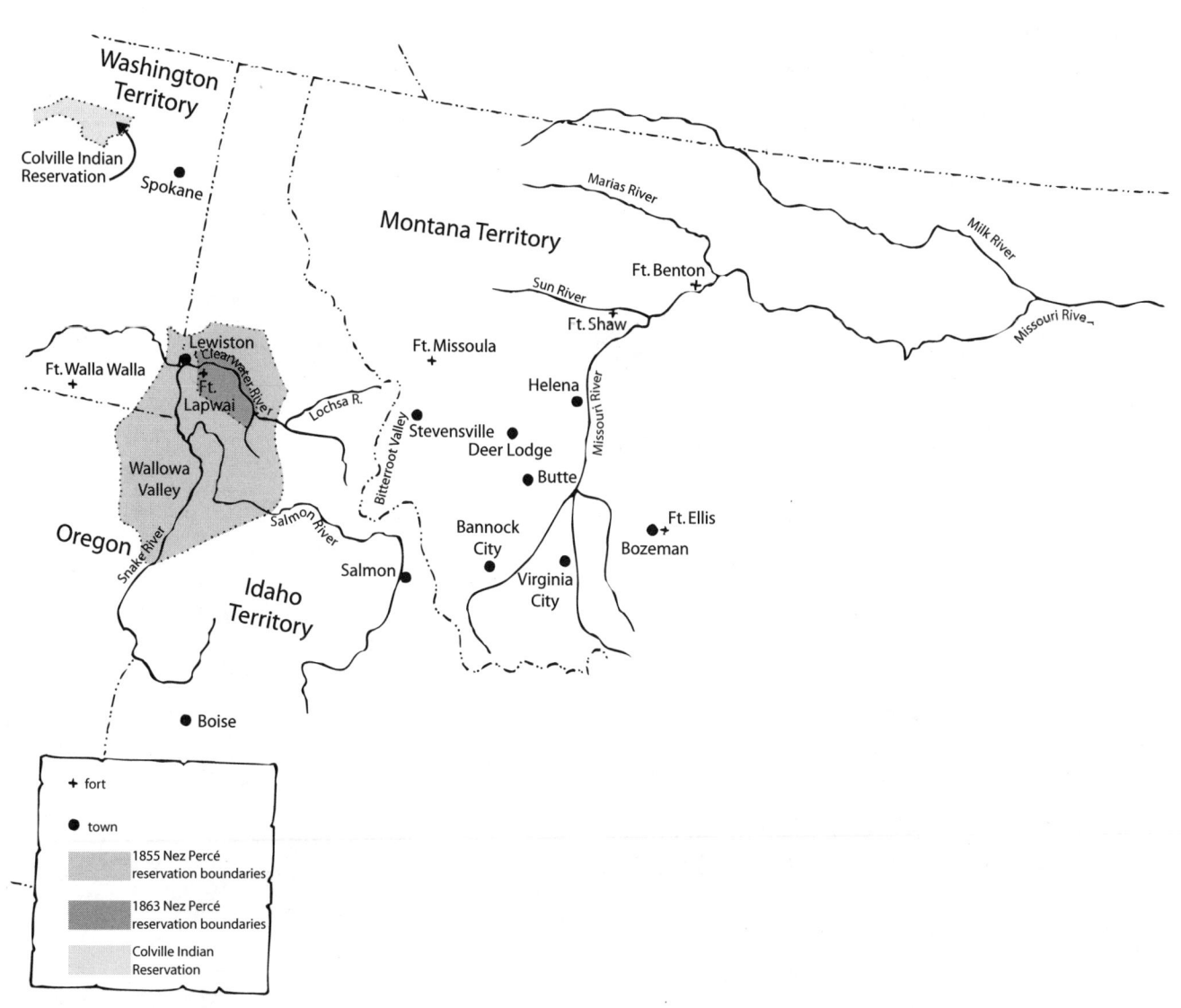

Handout 2

Time Line

1876 Chief Lawyer dies. General Oliver Otis Howard advises government officials that he believes that Young Chief Joseph and the non-treaty Nez Percé are legally entitled to the Wallowa Valley. United States policy is to move the Nez Percé and open the lands for settlement. Obeying government orders, Howard moves troops into the valley.

June 17: White Bird Battle

The Nez Percé, after first trying to negotiate a truce, attack Captain David Perry's troops in White Bird Canyon. The Nez Percé, under Young Chief Joseph's leadership, are successful.

July 1: Attack on Looking Glass' Village

Troops under the command of Captain Stephen Whipple attack Looking Glass' village. Though Looking Glass and his band of followers had not initially joined in with Young Chief Joseph, they join the war.

1877

May At the Lapwai Council, Young Chief Joseph tells General Oliver Otis Howard and others that the Wallowa Valley belongs to the Nez Percé, the homeland of their fathers, and that they are not going to leave. Troops are brought in to force the Nez Percé to relocate to the Lapwai Reservation in Idaho. Too-hool-hool-zote, Nez Percé wise man and war leader, is locked up. General Howard orders the Nez Percé to relocate to Lapwai within 30 days. Young Chief Joseph leads the non-treaty Nez Percé on a 1000-mile flight away from the United States Army.

Time Line

August 9: Big Hole Battle

According to a *New York Times* article that appeared September 20, 1877, "The best estimate of the strength of the [Nez Percé] gave them 260 warriors well armed and equipped, By forced marches Colonel (John) Gibbon came up with them with a command of 17 officers, 132 men and 34 citizens. The attack was made late at night, the [Nez Percé] being completely surprised, but as they immediately sought the bushes for shelter and poured their volleys into the troops as the latter came into the open ground, they did considerable execution. However, in 20 minutes the whole camp was in possession of the troops. The [Nez Percé] being driven out still fired with deadly effect at long range. By change of base shelter was obtained and retaliatory firing was commenced with equal destruction of [Nez Percé] life. The [Nez Percé] in the meantime captured the howitzer which was coming under escort and on a mule's back, the few privates who were with it fleeing incontinently and leaving the officers to an unequal fight. During the day various stratagems were employed, but it was 11 o'clock at night before the [Nez Percé] finally withdrew. On the 11th the dead were buried . . . 20 killed and 40 wounded. The burial party reported 83 dead [Nez Percé] found on the field and 6 more found dead in a ravine some distance from the battle-field."

Handout 2

Time Line

(modern state and international boundaries)

August 20 Camas Meadows
Ollokot and Looking Glass lead a Nez Percé war party to attack General Howard.

September 13: Battle of Canyon Creek
The cavalry charge a band of Nez Percé warriors at the mouth of Canyon Creek. The Nez Percé stop an army advance. Within days of the battle at Canyon Creek, the Nez Percé decide to head for Canada to join Sitting Bull.

September 30-October 5: Bear Paw Battle: The Surrender
According to an article that appeared in the *San Francisco Chronicle*, on Friday October 12, 1877,

Young Chief Joseph and his band of non-treaty Nez Percé surrender. "The capitulation of the entire band of Nez Percés under Joseph occurred at 2 o'clock on the afternoon of October 5th. The [Nez Percés] gave up their guns and ammunition, passing

Time Line

in review before General Miles and accepting an unconditional surrender . . . After the [Nez Percé] camp had been surrounded and the soldiers had secured defensive positions, only four casualties occurred. The soldiers closed in . . . slowly but surely the first day, all the time extending their line of rifle pits. It was the purpose of General Miles to lose no men in the attack. On the fourth day of the fight Joseph raised a white flag for the third time, and through an interpreter offered to surrender, provided they were allowed to keep their guns. Miles sent word that he must surrender without reserve, and the battle was again renewed. The white flag was displayed again on the fifth and last day, when JOSEPH APPEARED IN FRONT of his lines and advanced to meet Miles, to whom he tendered his gun. He was followed by 60 warriors, who also turned over their arms and shook hands with Miles. When the troops entered the rifle pits, 40 warriors were discovered disabled by wounds. They were removed to the camp hospital. The number of (Nez Percé) killed is not known, as they had already buried their dead. Miles left at noon on Sunday for Tongue River, taking with him his dead and wounded and the surrendered band. General Sturgis did not arrive in time to take a hand in the fight, and the glory of the victory rests with Miles. Howard, with an escort of 17 men, arrived on the field on the morning of the surrender. His presence there was not understood, and he made no attempt to assume command. He left his infantry at the Missouri River. And with his cavalry proceeded to the scene of the battle. The entrenchments occupied by the Indians consisted in all of over 160 rifle pits, which communicated with each other, so that assistance could be rendered if necessary. The squaws fought by the side of the warriors, and took care of the wounded and buried the dead."

Eighty-six men, 184 women and 147 children surrendered with Young Chief Joseph.

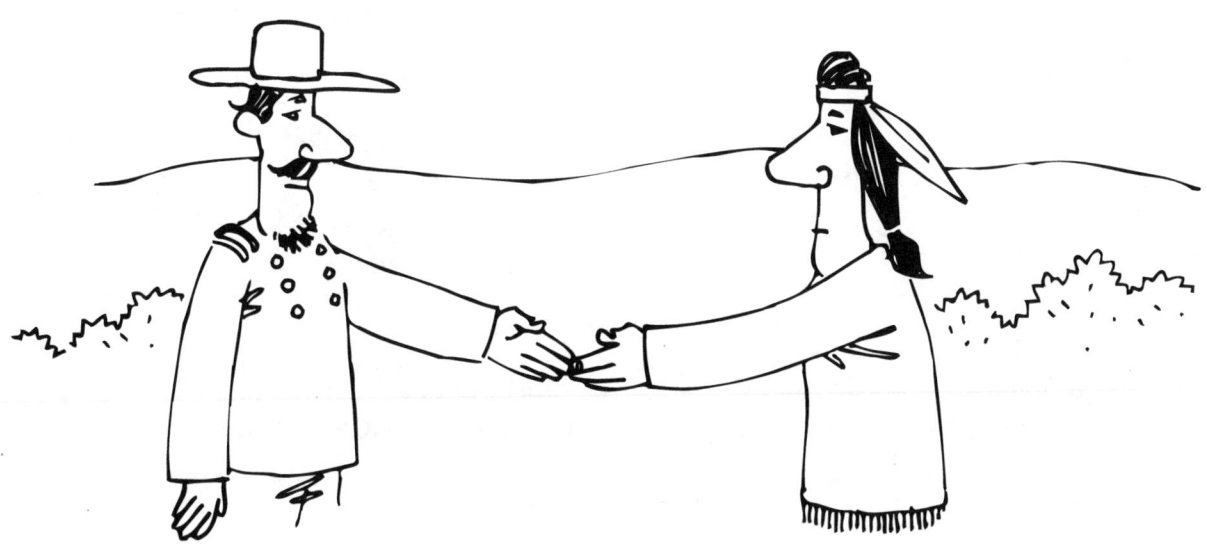

Handout 2

Time Line

November 27   Against the promises made by General Howard at the surrender, Chief Joseph and the Nez Percé are not returned to the northwest, but instead shipped by train to Fort Leavenworth, Kansas.

1878   Young Chief Joseph and his people are moved to Quapaw Reservation in Kansas.

1885   Chief Joseph and the non-treaty Nez Percé are relocated back to the northwest on the Colville Reservation in eastern Washington.

1904   Chief Joseph dies at the Colville Reservation in Washington.

Handout 2

Name _____

Time Line Activity

Look at the list of events below. Then write the event next to the year that it took place.

- Old Chief Joseph dies and his son, Joseph, becomes the leader of the Wallowa band of Nez Percé.

- Indian subagent, Dr. Elijah White, coerces the Nez Percé to accept Ellis as chief of all of the Nez Percé.

- Young Chief Joseph leads the non-treaty Nez Percé on a 1000-mile flight away from the United States Army. Surrenders October 5.

- Young Chief Joseph dies.

- Gold is discovered on the Nez Percé lands.

- The first treaty between the United States government and the Nez Percé signed.

- Non-treaty Nez Percé are moved from Kansas back to the northwest.

- Meriwether Lewis and William Clark meet the Nez Percé.

- A second treaty is negotiated. Old Chief Joseph abandons the talks. A treaty is signed by Chief Lawyer.

1805 _____

1842 _____

1855 _____

1860 _____

1863 _____

1871 _____

1877 _____

1885 _____

1904 _____

Handout 3

Name _____

Time Line Questions

1. Who were the first explorers to have contact with the Nez Percé? _____
   _____

2. What mission were the explorers on when they first made contact with the Nez Percé?
   _____

3. What did the explorers call the Nez Percé? _____
   _____

4. What do the Nez Percé call themselves and what does it mean? _____
   _____

5. How did the name *Nez Percé* come about? _____
   _____

6. List two things that brought settlers into contact with the Nez Percé. _____
   _____

7. How long had the Nez Percé lived in the Wallowa Valley? _____
   _____

8. Why did Young Chief Joseph leave the Wallowa Valley? _____
   _____

9. Who led the U. S. troops against the non-treaty Nez Percé? _____
   _____

10. Where did the surrender of the Nez Percé take place? _____
    _____

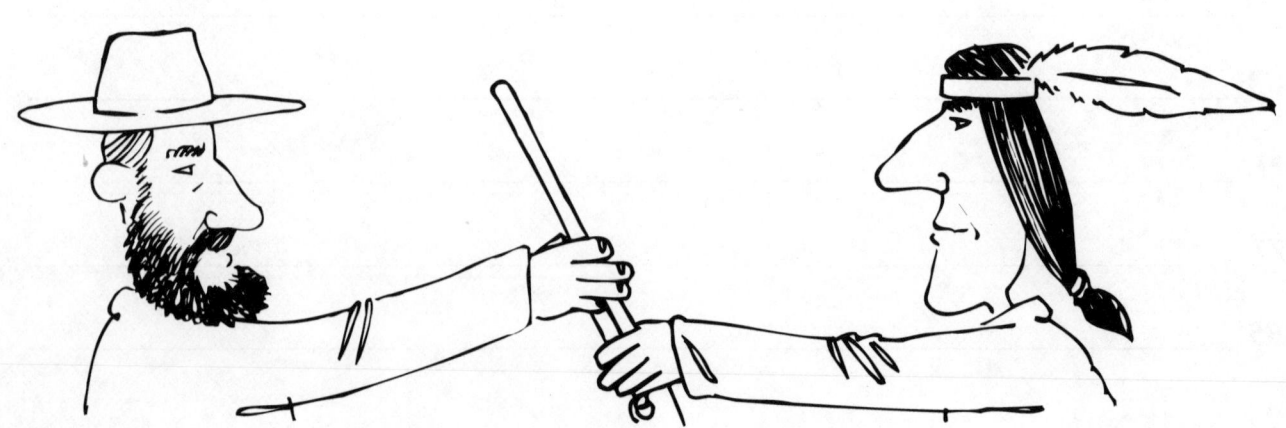

18 Handout 4

TLC10348 Copyright © Teaching & Learning Company, Carthage, IL 62321-0010

Name _____

Who's Who? Matching

Write the letter that best describes each person below.

a. Tuekakas
b. Hin-mah-too-yah-lat-kekht
c. Ollokot
d. Too-hool-hool-zote
e. Looking Glass
f. Dr. Elijah White
g. Chief Ellis
h. Chief Lawyer
i. Henry and Eliza Spalding
j. General Oliver Otis Howard

_____ 1. Nez Percé wise man and war leader

_____ 2. acknowledged as Nez Percé chief because he could speak English

_____ 3. Protestant missionaries

_____ 4. Young Chief Joseph

_____ 5. Nez Percé war chief

_____ 6. Young Chief Joseph's brother

_____ 7. Commanded U. S. troops

_____ 8. Old Chief Joseph

_____ 9. Succeeded Ellis as chief

_____ 10. Indian subagent

Define the following Nez Percé words and names:

1. Nee-Me-Poo _____

2. Ollokot _____

3. Hin-mah-too-yah-lat-kekht _____

4. Shugan _____

5. Khapkhaponimi _____

Handout 5

Name _____

Map Test

Label the following:

Columbia River	Snake River	Missouri River	Milk River
Yellowstone River	Bighorn River	Idaho	Oregon
Montana	Wyoming	Washington	Nevada
Utah	Colorado	Canada	Nez Percé Indian Reservation

Battles

| White Bird | Big Hole | Camas Meadows | Canyon Creek |
| Snake Creek | | | |

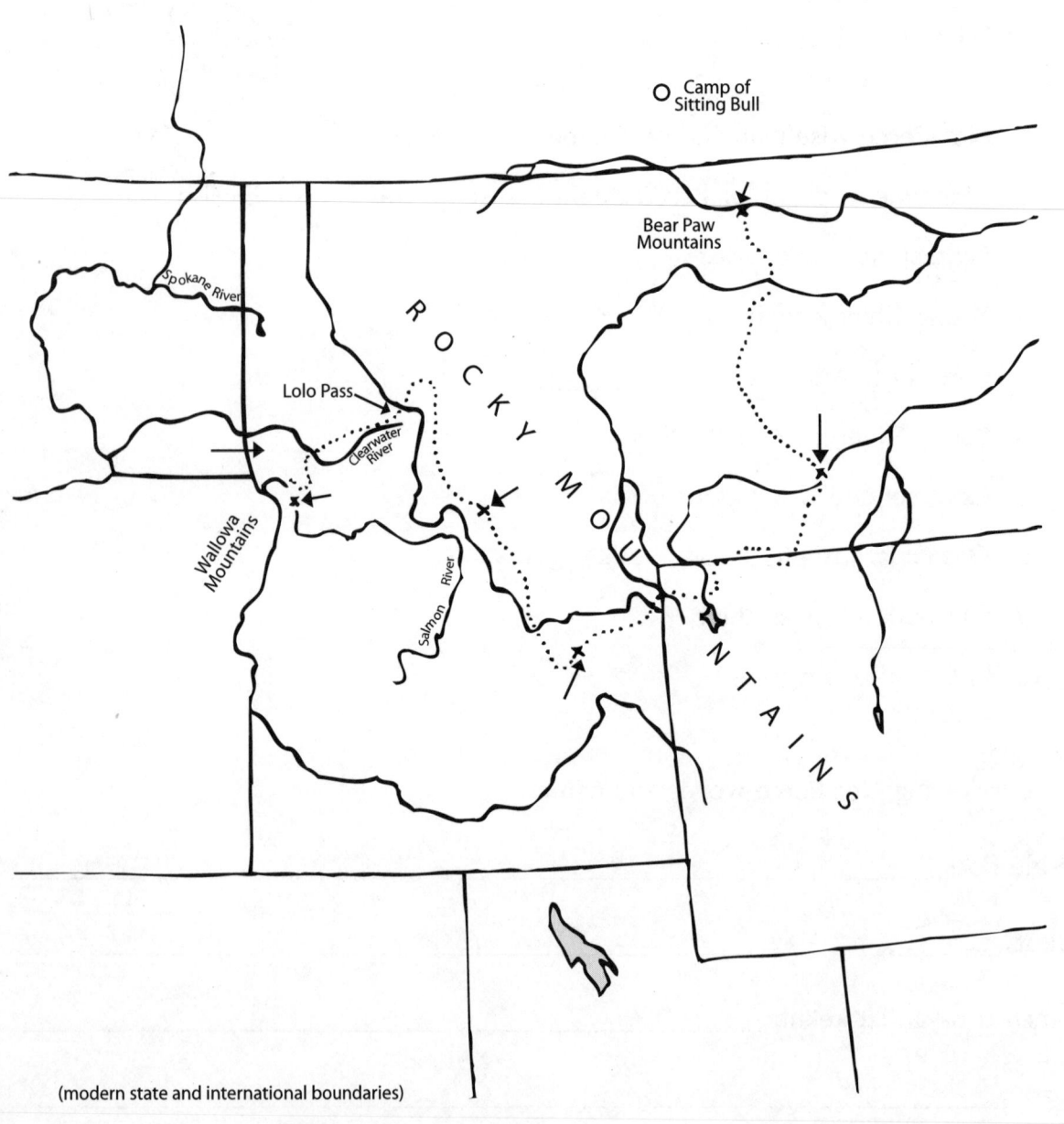

(modern state and international boundaries)

20   Handout 6   TLC10348 Copyright © Teaching & Learning Company, Carthage, IL 62321-0010

Chief Joseph's Surrender Speech

Objectives

To understand the significance of the speech

To identify the reasons for the Nez Percé surrender

To analyze the speech for facts, references and meaning

People to Look For

General Oliver O. Howard—One-armed army general famous for fighting Indians

Looking Glass—Great Nez Percé warrior

He Who Led the Young Men—Chief Joseph's brother, Ollokot

Too-hool-hool-zote—Nez Percé wise man and war leader

Background

After eluding U.S. troops for hundreds of miles the end of the chase came at Bear Paw, a four-day long battle in a blinding snowstorm. Young Chief Joseph knew that he was outnumbered and many of his people had died on the battlefield. He was surrounded and many of his family members and tribespeople were starving and freezing to death. General Howard's troops had begun shelling cannon artillery into the Nez Percé encampment. Young Chief Joseph knew it was over. With about 40 miles to go to the Canadian border and freedom, Young Chief Joseph and the non-treaty Nez Percé surrendered.

Suggested Lesson Plan

1. Explain the objectives of the lesson to the students.
2. Distribute copies of Chief Joseph's surrender speech.
3. Invite a student to read the contents of the speech aloud to the class.
4. Invite the students to discuss the speech.
5. Distribute copies of the speech review questions and invite the students to answer the questions.

To the Teacher

Chief Joseph's Surrender Speech at Bear Paw Battle—October 5, 1877

"Tell **General Howard** I know his heart. What he told me before I have in my heart.

I am tired of fighting, **Looking Glass** is dead. **Too-hool-hool-zote** is dead. The old men are all dead. It is the young men who say yes or no. **He who led the young men** is dead. It is cold, and we have no blankets. The little children are freezing to death. My people, some of them, have run away to the hills and have no blankets, no food. No one knows where they are—perhaps freezing to death. I want to have time to look for my children and see how many of them I can find. Maybe I shall find them among the dead.

Hear me, my chiefs. I am tired. My heart is sick and sad. From where the sun now stands, I will fight no more forever."

Name _____

Chief Joseph's Surrender Speech at Bear Paw Battle—October 5, 1877 Review

1. To whom does Chief Joseph surrender? _____
2. Who is Looking Glass? _____
3. Who is Too-hool-hool-zote? _____
4. Who is He Who Led the Young Men? _____
5. What does Chief Joseph say about fighting? _____
   _____
6. What does Chief Joseph say about his people? _____
   _____
7. What does Chief Joseph say about his own children? _____
   _____
8. What does Chief Joseph say to his chiefs? _____
   _____
9. Describe the tone of the speech. _____
   _____
10. Is the speech more emotional or more logical in tone? Explain your answer. _____
    _____
    _____

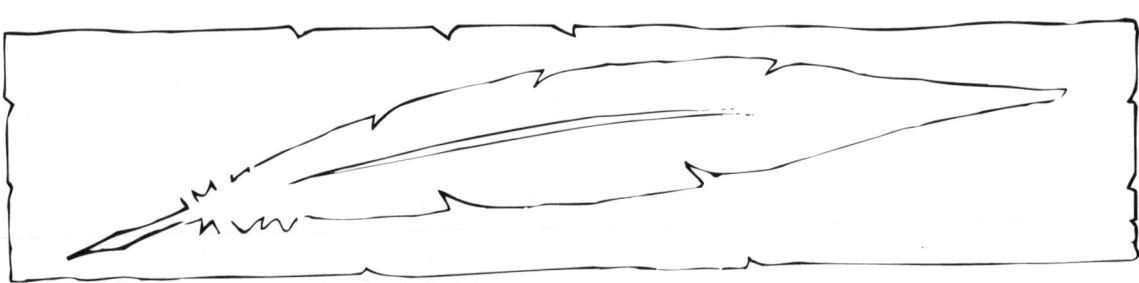

Handout 8

Editorial Writing

Objectives

To recognize the difference between opinion and fact in newspaper writing

To compare two news stories

To identify fact, bias and opinion

To judge the opinion of an editorial

To write one's own editorial

Vocabulary

opinion: A belief based not on absolute certainty or positive knowledge but on what seems true, valid or probable to one's own mind; judgment

fact: Something that is true, can be proven to be true

Background

George Horne wrote, "A newspaper is the history for one day of the world in which we live . . . ." So, provided here is a snapshot of what happened when Chief Joseph surrendered and one article providing an opinion about the war. Following are the two articles from two newspapers—the *San Francisco Chronicle* and the *New York Times*—from 1877. The *Chronicle* article is typical of 19th century newspaper articles, including numerous headlines, accounts of the events from other newspapers and reprints of official dispatches with little narrative to tell the story. However, the story does deliver the traditional five Ws—who, what, where, when, why—and the how. The second article—from the *Times*—expresses the opinion that the Nez Percé War was unjust.

To the Teacher

Editorial Writing

Suggested Lesson Plan

1. Explain the objectives of the lesson to the students.
2. Define the vocabulary, the difference between opinion and fact.
3. As practice for the students differentiating fact from opinion, ask the students which of the following statements are true and which are opinions:
   a. Franklin Roosevelt was the greatest President of the twentieth century.
   Franklin Roosevelt was President of the United States from 1933 to 1945.
   Franklin Roosevelt served longer as President than any other person elected to the presidency.
   Franklin Roosevelt was the most popular President in American history.
   Franklin Roosevelt married his cousin Eleanor Roosevelt.
   Franklin Roosevelt was distantly related to President Theodore Roosevelt.
   b. *Moby Dick* is the greatest American novel ever written.
   Moby Dick was written by Herman Melville.
   Moby Dick is about Captain Ahab and a whale.
   Moby Dick was first published in 1851.
4. Distribute copies of the *San Francisco Chronicle* article and the *New York Times* editorial. Do not tell the students which is the news article and which is the editorial. Ask the students to judge the two articles and offer their opinions about which is the editorial and which is the news article. Remind the students to be looking for facts and opinions in the articles. Ask them to circle opinions in each article with a red pen, and circle facts in each article with a blue pen.
5. After the students have had time to read the two articles, ask them which is the editorial and which is the news article. Ask the students to explain their answers. Possible answers could include: The *San Francisco Chronicle* article has headlines; the *New York Times* article expresses opinions and says so in the article—"We freely express the opinion that the Nez Percé war was, on the part of our Government, an unpardonable and frightful blunder—a crime, whose victims are alike the hundreds of our gallant officers and men who fell a prey to Nez Percé bullets and the peaceful bands who were goaded by injustice and wrong to the war-path."
6. Ask the students if they agree or disagree with the *New York Times* editorial. Invite the students to write an editorial of their own expressing their opinions about the Nez Percé War.
7. Distribute the activity sheets for each of the articles and ask the students to answer the questions.

To the Teacher

25

San Francisco Chronicle, Wednesday, October 10, 1877

[1]

AT LAST! Chief Joseph Surrenders To General Miles.

End of the Campaign Against The Nez Percés.

General Howard Hears and Reports the News.

Particulars of Miles' Fight With The Indians.

A Three-Day Battle in a Blinding Snowstorm.

(Special Dispatches to the *Chronicle*.)

CHICAGO, October 9.—The following dispatch was received at headquarters today: DISTRICT OF THE YELLOWSTONE, CAMP ON EAGLE CREEK, MONTANA

General A. H. Terry

[2]
October 5, 1877.

General A. H. Terry, Commanding the Department of Dakota—Dear General: We have had our usual success. We made a very direct and rapid march across the country, and after a severe engagement, and being kept under fire for three days, the hostile camp of Nez Percé under Chief Joseph surrendered at 9 o'clock to-day. I intend to start the Second Cavalry toward Benton on the 7th instant. Cannot supplies be sent out on the Benton road to meet them, and return with the remainder of the command to the Yellowstone? I hear that there is trouble between the Sioux and the Canadian authorities. I remain, General, yours very truly, Nelson A Miles, Colonel, Brevet-General, U.S.A., Commanding.

San Francisco Chronicle,
Wednesday, October 10, 1877

[3]
Another Account

HELENA, (Mont.), October 9—The *Fort Benton Record* published the following extras, dated October 8th. 2 A. M.: J. J. Healy arrived from Miles command this morning with official dispatches to General Terry, announcing the surrender of Joseph and his band, numbering about 850 men, women, and children, on the 5th instant, at 9 P. M.

General A.H. Terry

[4]
General Howard Heard From.

The following dispatch, dated "In the field, Miles commanding, Eagle Creek, Montana, October 5th," and signed by General O. O. Howard, was received at military headquarters in this city last night: "The hostile Nez Percé under Chief Joseph surrendered to-day at 2:20 p.m. Most of the principal chiefs were killed in the engagement of the 30th ——, including Looking Glass, Joseph's brother, and Tahoolhooshute. The late ——Prairie murderers are all now dead, killed in action."

[5]
General Miles Fight with Joseph.

HELENA, (Montana). October 9—I have received the following details of General Miles fight: On the afternoon of September 28th Major Ingles sent a courier from Cow Island to inform General Miles the direction the Indians have taken on the 29th of September. The courier reached Miles' command. Miles being informed of the direction of the Indians moved rapidly to the upper or northern Bear Paw and struck the Nez Percé camp on the 30th on a tributary of Snake Creek. It was snowing hard at the time and he got within two miles of the camp before the Indians discovered him. Immediately on the discovery Miles pushed his worn horses into a trot, then a gallop, which ended in a fierce charge as he neared the Indians, who were partially entrenched in rifle-pits. In the charge Miles lost heavily in men and horses, but he captured a herd of Indian horses and killed and wounded many Indians.

General Miles

Handout 9

San Francisco Chronicle, Wednesday, October 10, 1877

[6]
Killed and Wounded Many Indians.

The Indians held to the rifle-pits, and Miles being unable to charge them out, encircled the entrenched Indians, placing his men fifteen feet apart, and then opened fire with two pieces of artillery. Joseph then raised the white flag and came to Miles' headquarters on the evening of the 30th, when a truce was observed. During the night of the 30th and the morning of the 1st, Miles occupied his time in caring for his wounded and in strengthening his grasp on the Indians, and the Indians occupied their time in digging more rifle-pits and drifting — —from one pit to another. During the truce Joseph remained in Miles' tent, and Miles sent some of the whites into Indian camp to explore it, one of whom, Lieutenant Jerome, they held as a hostage for the return of Joseph. On the afternoon of October 1st the fight was renewed and continued during the night and the day of the 2nd. An exchange was then affected—Lieutenant Jerome for Joseph.

Lt. Jerome

[7]
The Fight Went On.

The courier left on the night of the 3rd, and on the morning of the 4th he could still hear cannonading. There was not a stick of timber near the camp of Miles, and there was much suffering among the wounded for the want of fires. Miles sent his pack animals to the mountains for wood, but a blinding snow storm rendered it impossible for men to follow their course, and a tedious delay occurred before fuel was procured. The number of horses captured from the Indians is estimated at 700.

Name _____

San Francisco Chronicle, Wednesday, October 10, 1877 Matching

Read the excerpt from the "*San Francisco Chronicle*, Wednesday, October 10, 1877," and answer the following questions.

____ 1. Nelson Miles
____ 2. Looking Glass
____ 3. Chief Joseph
____ 4. General Terry
____ 5. Lieutenant Jerome

a. Led the non-treaty Nez Percé into war
b. was traded for Chief Joseph
c. Commanding general of the Dakotas
d. Chief Joseph's brother
e. General commanding the battle against Chief Joseph

____ 6. According to the article's headlines, who won the battle?

7. How long did the battle last? _____

8. What weather conditions hampered the battle? _____

9. In paragraph 2, what is General Miles asking for? _____

10. From what newspaper did the account of the surrender come? _____

11. Who was Looking Glass? _____

12. Who was exchanged for the captured Chief Joseph? _____

13. What strategy employed by General Miles finally won the battle? _____

14. According to the article, how many Nez Percé were captured? _____

15. Where did the final battle take place? _____

Handout 10

29

New York Times, Monday, October 15, 1877

A Lesson from the Nez Percé

[1]
Now that the Nez Percé war has ended in victory, thanks to the energy and courage of our much-enduring Army, it is worth while, before it passes out of mind, to ask why it was fought. We freely express the opinion that the Nez Percé war was, on the part of our Government, an unpardonable and frightful blunder—a crime, whose victims are alike the hundreds of our gallant officers and men who fell a prey to Nez Percé bullets and the peaceful bands who were goaded by injustice and wrong to the war-path. It is greatly to be regretted that the immediate responsibility for its occurrence is so obscurely distributed that it is difficult to bring anybody to account for it at the bar of public opinion.

[2]
The Nez Percé comes into history as the white man's friend. The famous exploring party sent out by President Jefferson said of this tribe: "The Pierced-Nose nation are among the most amiable men we have seen—stout, well-formed, well-looking, active, their character placid and gentle, rarely moved into passion, yet not often enlivened by gayety." From their first warm welcome of our explorers in 1805, up to the present war, no full-blooded Nez Percé is known to have murdered a white man—an extraordinary fact which is on record in the Government archives in Washington. With the Nez Percés we have always been at peace; and when we have had wars with other neighboring tribes, the Nez Percés have invariably been the allies of our Army. While other tribes have been roving and hard to control, a large part of the Nez Percés have taken to grazing and farming. Most of them live in houses like white men, and build fences around their lands. The brother of Chief Lawyer is a Presbyterian minister in Oregon. These harmless and peaceful neighbors, these faithful allies in every war, were the nation that we have drove to desperation and deeds of blood.

New York Times, Monday, October 15, 1877

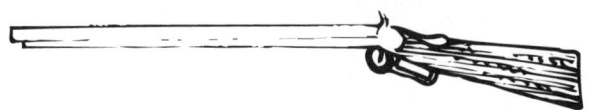

[3]

When white men first found them, the Nez Percés had bands, but no general chief—a system often, if not always, found among Indians west of the Rocky Mountains. Thirty-five years ago the United States Indian Agent for that region undertook to remedy this, which in his wisdom he conceived to be a defect, by giving them a grand chief named ELLIS, whose main recommendation was that he had learned English at a mission and so could talk to the agent. Less peaceful Indians than the Nez Percés might have gone to war rather than agree to the agent's labor-saving contrivance. The Nez Percés protested, but waited patiently for ELLIS' death, when, however, they were pressed to choose a new general chief. The rivalry lay between JOSEPH, a scion of the most illustrious Nez Percés, the father of the present JOSEPH, and an Indian named LAWYER. As LAWYER, like ELLIS, knew English, he received the powerful support of the Government agents, who gave him an enormous advantage by conducting all their business with the Nez Percés through him. JOSEPH's father at length withdrew in disgust from the councils of his tribe, still claiming the headship, if there were to be any.

[4]

The dwelling place of the Nez Percés, as far back as their tradition goes, has been the Wallowa Valley, prized by them for its roots and its fishing, and now for its grazing. The whites at length began to increase in numbers, and, of course, took measures to dispossess the Indians of the valley. For this purpose they framed the successive treaties of 1855, 1863, and 1868, providing the Nez Percé Reservation and annuities instead of their lands. Old Chief JOSEPH, however, refused to go upon the reservation, and remained, with his band and the other non-treaty Nez Percés, so called, in the Wallowa Valley, rightly claiming that the rest of the tribe had no right to give it up to the United States and white settlers as against the non-treaty Indians, because it was held in common. It should be said here that the present Chief JOSEPH insists that his father never signed any of these treaties; that this was his father's instruction to him, and that the fact that their band remained away from the reservation shows it. But the Government is said to be able to show that JOSEPH reluctantly signed the treaty of 1855. Admitting this latter statement to be correct, as we have no doubt that it is yet the treaty which definitely undertook to give up the Wallowa Valley was that of 1863, and this most unquestionably old JOSEPH did not sign, as he also did not sign the treaty of 1868. He died in 1871.

New York Times, Monday, October 15, 1877

[5]

The claim of JOSEPH to his ancestral homestead was, therefore, good, prima facie—so good, at any rate, that there was no case for driving him out with the bayonet. Even the treaty Indians could almost have claimed to have the Wallowa Valley restored to them, for it is proved beyond any doubt that the Government never carried out its stipulations for land partition, which formed an essential part of the treaties. The Government, however, holds with reason that the continued acceptance of the benefits of the treaties partly meets that objection as regards them; and for the non-treaty bands, off the reservation, another means has been found—coercion, violence, and a bloody war.

[6]

Now, these are not fancy sketches or rumors; they are officially-ascertained facts, well known to the Government, and they are to be found in two admirably clear reports, drawn up and presented to the Government more than a year ago, by no less an authority than Col. H. CLAY WOOD, a staff officer of Gen. HOWARD himself. They are the result of most careful investigations, and one of Col. WOOD'S conclusions in a later report was that the present JOSEPH and his band have in law an undivided interest in all lands ceded to the United States by the treaty of 1863, though he only claimed the Wallowa Valley, or rather the tract of land set apart by President GRANT'S order of 1873.

New York Times, Monday, October 15, 1877

[7]

A brief reference to this last order must close the story. Settlers having begun to encroach on the non-treaty Indian lands, in June, 1873, President GRANT ordered that these possessions should be "withheld from entry and settlement as public lands, and that the same be set apart as a reservation for the roaming Nez Percé Indians, as recommended by the Secretary of the Interior and the Commissioner of Indian Affairs." The decision took the form of an order, because no treaties are allowed since the act of 1871. JOSEPH continued, therefore, with his band to peacefully occupy his ancestral home in the Wallowa Valley under an order which warned off others from interfering with his rights. Two years ago President GRANT issued another order summarily revoking the former, and saying that "the said described tract of country is hereby restored to the public domain." The settlers at once encroached; the Government ordered the non-treaty Nez Percés to go upon the reservation; to their pleadings against the injustice, the menacing reply was the gathering of troops which the Indian Department called for, in order, if necessary, to put them on by force. Just before the time set for executing this scheme, JOSEPH, who had held back for months, and to the last moment, from a resort to which peaceful Nez Percés were repugnant. At length counseling with his brother non-treaty chiefs, and seeing soldiers assembled to drive him from his home, desperately plunged into war—a war which, on our part, was in its origin and motive nothing short of a gigantic blunder and a crime.

Name _____

New York Times Editorial, Monday, October 15, 1877 Review

Read the editorial from the *New York Times* and answer the following questions:

1. In paragraph 1, what opinion did the *Times* express about the war with the Nez Percé?
   _____
   _____

2. According to the editorial, how long had the Nez Percé been the "white man's" friend?
   _____
   _____

3. Why, according to the editorial, did the United States government want to take the land away from the Nez Percé? _____
   _____

4. Who was Ellis? _____

5. Who was Lawyer? _____

6. In paragraph 6, who does the editorialist claim as a source of information? _____
   _____

7. In your opinion, why would the editorialist provide the source of information in the editorial? _____
   _____

8. What four reasons are listed in the editorial as reasons that the war against the Nez Percé was unjust? _____
   _____

9. What does the editorialist express, in paragraph 7, as Chief Joseph's reason for going to war? _____
   _____

10. How did President Ulysses Grant's 1875 order affect Chief Joseph's decision? _____
    _____

34   Handout 12

Editorial Cartoons

Objectives

To identify caricature

To identify symbolism

To draw conclusions about the meaning in an editorial cartoon

To identify stereotyping

To identify racism

To draw one's own editorial cartoons

To judge a cartoonist's viewpoint

Vocabulary

caricature: A drawing of a person that uses exaggerated features

symbolism: When one thing (symbol) stands for or represents something else
Examples: the Liberty Bell symbolizes freedom; the flag symbolizes the U. S.; the golden arches symbolize McDonald's®

stereotyping: A general, oversimplified view held by members of a group about another group that does not allow for a difference of opinion about individuals, and is usually prejudiced

Know-Nothing: This was a political party that sprang up in the mid-19th century as a reaction to a wave of Irish immigrants who were mainly Roman Catholic. The Know-Nothings believed that the Catholics were subservient to the Pope and not the founding principles of the American government. They believed that the Irish immigrants were going to stop the American political experiment. This group sought to limit immigration and the rights of immigrants.

satire: Using ridicule, sarcasm and irony to attack follies and abuses

irony: To say one thing, but mean another

Example:

The Crocodile
by Lewis Carroll

How doth the little crocodile
Improve his shining tail,
And pour the waters of the Nile
On every golden scale!
How cheerfully he seems to grin,
How neatly spreads his claws,
And welcomes little fishes in,
With gently smiling jaws!

To the Teacher **35**

Editorial Cartoons

Background

Editorial cartoons make their editorial comments through art rather than writing. Even though most editorial cartoons contain writing, most of the message is to be found in the art. The cartoonist relies on the reader to understand the visual message in the cartoon. For this to happen, the reader has to be familiar with the story and the events relating to the cartoon.

The two editorial cartoons included in this book were drawn by Thomas Nast, the best-known and most widely published American cartoonist in the 19th century. Nast will forever be remembered as the cartoonist who gave the two American political parties their emblems, the Republican elephant and the Democratic donkey. He is also remembered for fixing two images in the American pantheon of symbolism—the fat and jolly Santa Claus and the tall, lanky and thinly bearded Uncle Sam.

Nast was born in 1840 in Landau, Germany, and emigrated with his parents to the United States as a small boy. Nast was not a great student, only being interested in art. As luck would have it, Nast was discovered by *Leslie's Weekly* magazine. He began his career as an illustrator, but within a few years he was drawing cartoons for which he gained fame. In 1862 he joined the staff at *Harper's Weekly* magazine and continued to draw for them for the next 25 years.

The two cartoons included in this book were drawn in the 1870s in *Harper's Weekly*, a picture magazine with nearly 300,000 subscribers. Both cartoons portray Nast's feelings about the mistreatment of Native Americans. Nast was a liberal Republican who believed that all citizens should have equal rights. Nast was a champion for the rights of minority groups, as both of these cartoons can attest.

Editorial Cartoons

In "Every Dog" (No Distinction of Color) "Has His Day." Nast shows two men, a Native American and a Chinese immigrant, talking as they look at a wall full of posters. The posters are all anti-immigrant and express a sentiment that grew in America out of the waves of immigration that took place in the United States. The first big wave of immigrants included the Irish after the Irish potato famine of 1848 that caused thousands of Irish to come to America. The poster at the top of the cartoon depicts a train moving west and forcing out the Native Americans and a train going east bringing in the Chinese, who were brought to the United States to help build the railroads. The posters on the wall are clearly aimed at the Chinese—THE CHINESE MUST GO, THE CHINESE PROBLEM, PROHIBIT CHINESE IMMIGRATION, LAWS PROVIDING FOR THEIR BANISHMENT. But the posters also make it clear that the Chinese are not the only immigrant groups that must go—FOREIGNERS NOT WANTED, KNOW NOTHING OF THE PAST. DOWN WITH THE IRISH, DOWN WITH THE DUTCH. Clearly these posters apply to any group who recently immigrated. Nast uses irony superbly in this cartoon. Here the Native American counsels the Chinese immigrant, telling him that Native Americans were moved from their homelands by European Americans who moved west on the railroad, and that those same Americans were not going to be displaced by Chinese immigrants who were brought in as cheap laborers. Meanwhile in the background, an African American patiently sits waiting for his time to come—MY DAY IS COMING.

In "Move On!" a dark foreboding police officer waves his baton to stop a Native American from going to the voting booth. While in the background, Irish Americans, (Nast portrays them with shamrocks and pipes) who have been recently naturalized, are voting. The irony is that while Native Americans born on American soil are denied the right to vote, those who have recently immigrated to the United States have access to the ballot box and a voice in American politics. This cartoon portrays voting in the United States, considered a cornerstone to our democracy, as corrupt.

NOTE: These cartoons may be considered racist. Indeed, what Nast is pointing out is the deep prejudices that were common against the Native Americans, Chinese and other recent immigrant groups in the United States at the time. Some students may find them offensive. Use caution when introducing these cartoons to your class, and supervise and monitor the discussion.

To the Teacher

Editorial Cartoons

Suggested Lesson Plan

1. Explain the objectives of the lesson to the students.
2. Define the vocabulary.
3. Distribute copies of the "Every Dog" (No Distinction of Color) "Has His Day" (page 39) Nast editorial cartoon. Ask the students if the depiction of the Native American and the Chinese immigrant are stereotyped? Ask the students what literary devices—irony and satire—Nast is using in this cartoon.
4. Distribute the activity question handout (page 40).
5. Distribute copies of the "Move On!" (page 41) Nast editorial cartoon. Ask the students if Nast's portrayal of Irish immigrants is flattering.
6. Distribute copies of the handout (page 42) and invite the students to answer the questions.

"Every Dog" (No Distinction of Color) "Has His Day" Editorial Cartoon

"Every Dog" (No Distinction of Color) "Has His Day."
Red Gentleman to Yellow Gentleman. "Pale face 'fraid you crowd him out, as he did me."

From *Thomas Nast: Cartoons and Illustrations*, written by Thomas Nast St. Hill, Dover Publications, New York, published in 1974. Reprinted with permission from Dover Publications.

Name _____

"Every Dog" (No Distinction of Color) "Has His Day." Editorial Cartoon Questions

Look at the Thomas Nast cartoon and answer the following questions:

1. Who does the figure wearing the feathers represent? _____

2. Who does the figure wearing the hat in the foreground represent? _____

3. Who does the man in the background represent? _____

4. How do the words, "My Day Is Coming," relate to the man in the background? _____
   _____

5. Look at the poster displayed above the heads of the two men talking. How does the activity in the poster relate to the caption of the cartoon, "Pale face 'fraid you crowd him out, as he did me?'" _____
   _____

6. What role does the poster displayed above the two men's heads, assign to the railroad?
   _____
   _____

7. The American Know-Nothing Party flourished in the mid-19th century. One of its major political planks was the banning of immigration. In the poster at the feet of the two men speaking, how does this relate to the message in the cartoon? _____
   _____

8. According to the cartoon, what immigrant group is being discriminated against, and why?
   _____

9. What ethnic groups does this cartoon imply there have been discrimination against? Explain your answer. _____
   _____

10. Do you think the cartoonist is in favor of immigration or against it? Explain your answer.
    _____

40 Handout 14   TLC10348 Copyright © Teaching & Learning Company, Carthage, IL 62321-0010

"Move On!" Editorial Cartoon

"Move On!"

Has the Native Americans no rights that the naturalized American is bound to respect?

From *Thomas Nast: Cartoons and Illustrations*, written by Thomas Nast St. Hill, Dover Publications, New York, published in 1974. Reprinted with permission from Dover Publications.

Handout 15

Name _____

"Move On!" Editorial Cartoon Questions

Look at the cartoon and answer the questions below. (You may have to refer to other sources to answer some of these questions.)

1. In this cartoon, what activity is happening in the background? _____
   _____

2. What clues are there to support your answer to the first question? _____
   _____

3. How does the cartoonist portray the voting taking place? _____
   _____

4. Look for clues among the men who are voting. What nationality are they? Explain your answer. _____
   _____

5. What is the officer stopping the Native American from doing? _____

6. What clues does the cartoonist give the viewer that the officer is talking to a Native American? _____
   _____

7. Explain how the element of satire is used in this cartoon. _____
   _____

8. What is the message the cartoonist is making about the rights of the Native Americans versus naturalized citizens? _____
   _____

9. What is a naturalized citizen? _____
   _____

10. Is this cartoonist in favor of voting rights for Native Americans? Explain your answer.
    _____
    _____

Handout 16

Bibliography

Resources for Teachers

Freedman, Russell. *Indian Chiefs*. New York: Holiday House, 1987.

Gidley, M. (Mick) *KOPET: A Documentary Narrative of Chief Joseph's Last Years*. Seattle, Washington: University of Washington Press, 1981.

Greene, Jerome A. *Nez Percé Summer 1877: The U.S. Army and the Nee-Me-Poo Crisis*. Helena, Montana: Montana Historical Society Press, 2000.

Howard, Helen Addison. *Saga of Chief Joseph*. Lincoln, Nebraska: University of Nebraska Press, 1978.

St. Hill, Thomas Nast. *Thomas Nast: Cartoons and Illustrations*. New York: Dover Publications. 1974.

Bibliography

Suggested Books for Students

Howes, Kathi. *The Nez Percé*. Vero Beach, Florida: Rourke Publications, Inc., 1990.

Scott, Robert A. *Chief Joseph and the Nez Percés*. New York: Facts on File, 1993.

Taylor, Marian W. *Chief Joseph: Nez Percé Leader*. New York: Chelsea House Publishers, 1993.

Trafzer, Clifford E. *The Nez Percé*. New York: Chelsea House Publishers, 1992.

Yates, Diana. *Chief Joseph: Thunder Rolling Down from the Mountain*. Staten Island, New York: Ward Hill Press, 1992.

Answer Key

Time Line Activity, page 17

1805 Meriwether Lewis and William Clark meet the Nez Percé.
1842 Indian subagent, Dr. Elijah White, coerces the Nez Percé to accept Ellis as chief of all of the Nez Percé.
1855 The first treaty between the United States government and the Nez Percé signed.
1860 Gold is discovered on the Nez Percé lands.
1863 A second treaty is negotiated. Old Chief Joseph abandons the talks. A treaty is signed by Chief Lawyer.
1871 Old Chief Joseph dies and his son, Joseph, becomes the leader of the Wallowa band of Nez Percé.
1877 Young Chief Joseph leads the non-treaty Nez Percé on a 1000-mile flight away from the United States Army. Surrenders October 5.
1885 Non-treaty Nez Percé are moved from Kansas back to the northwest.
1904 Young Chief Joseph dies.

Time Line Questions, page 18

1. Lewis and Clark
2. exploring the continental United States on behalf of President Thomas Jefferson
3. Chopunnish
4. Nee-Me-Poo, "the people"
5. some Native Americans pierce their noses
6. the Oregon Trail, gold discovery
7. archaeologists believe 13,000 years
8. troops were forcing them to move to a reservation
9. General Howard
10. Bear Paw, Montana

Who's Who? Matching, page 19

1. D
2. G
3. I
4. B
5. E
6. C
7. J
8. A
9. H
10. F

Define the following Nez Percé words and names:

1. Nee-Me-Poo: "the people"
2. Ollokot: "frog"
3. Hin-mah-too-yah-lat-kekht: "thunder rolling down from the mountains"
4. Shugan: "brown"
5. Khapkhaponimi: "loose bark on a tree"

Answer Key

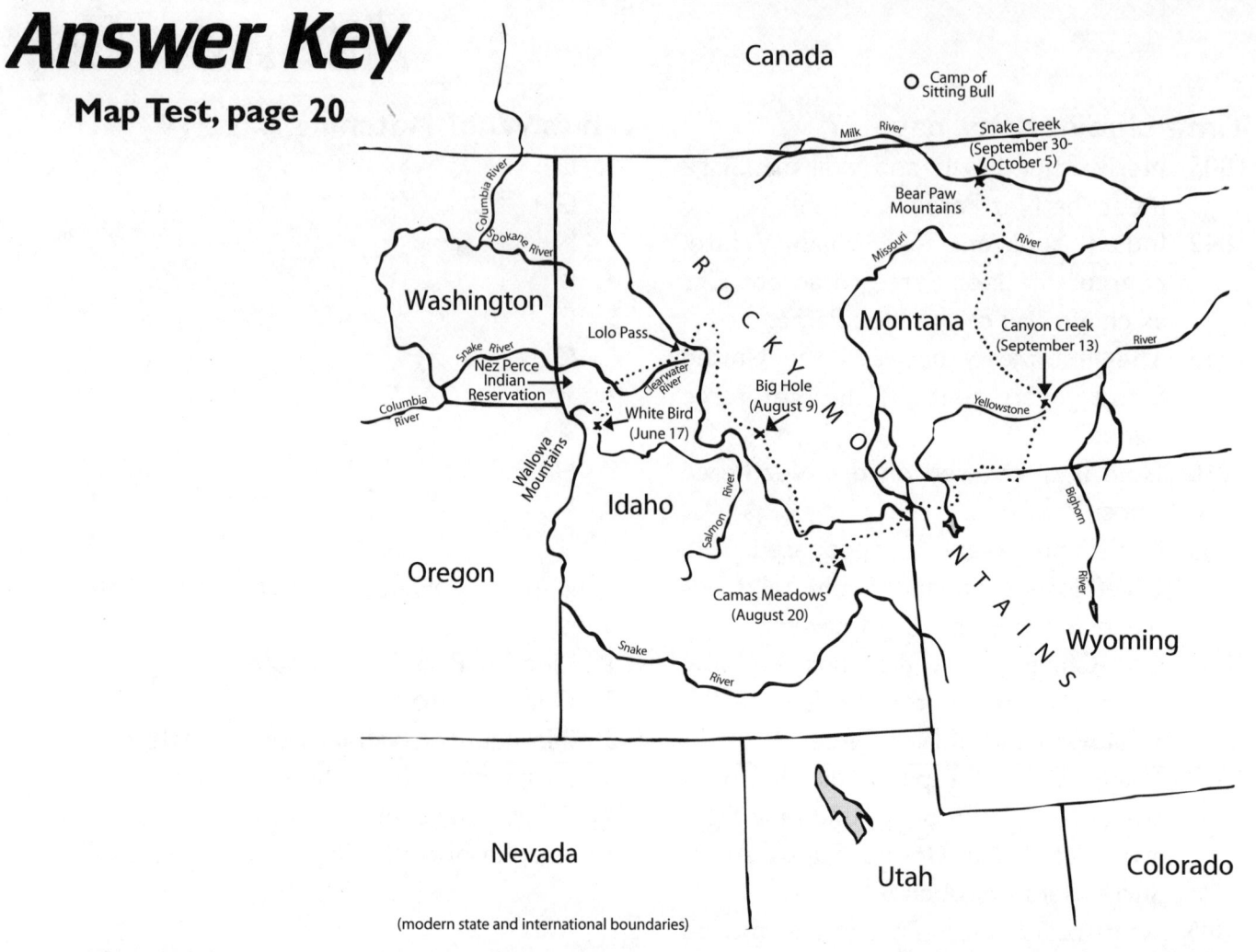

Map Test, page 20

Chief Joseph's Surrender Speech at Bear Paw Battle, October 5, 1877, page 23

1. General Howard
2. A Nez Percé war chief
3. A Nez Percé wise man
4. Chief Joseph's younger brother, Ollokot
5. Chief Joseph is tired of the fighting.
6. His people are cold and hungry.
7. Some of his children may be among the dead; he wants to look for them.
8. To listen to him because he is sick and sad.
9. Answers will vary but could include: the speech's tone is sad and mournful.
10. Answers will vary but could include: the speech is more emotional because Chief Joseph begins with talking about what is in his heart. He talks about how tired he is, how his heart is sick and sad.

San Francisco Chronicle, Wednesday, October 10, 1877 Matching, page 29

1. E
2. D
3. A
4. C
5. B
6. General Miles and his troops
7. three days
8. blinding snowstorm
9. supplies
10. *Fort Benton Record*
11. Looking Glass was a great Nez Percé warrior.
12. Lieutenant Jerome
13. To encircle the Nez Percé camp and bombard it with artillery
14. 850 Nez Percé men, women and children
15. Bear Paw, a tributary of Snake Creek, in Montana

Answer Key

New York Times Editorial, Monday October 15, 1877, page 34

1. The war was an unpardonable and frightful blunder and a crime.
2. Since the first explorers, Lewis and Clark, met them on their famous expedition in 1805
3. For white settlement
4. Ellis was a Nez Percé that the United States deemed to be a grand chief of the Nez Percé.
5. Lawyer was the successor to Chief Ellis.
6. Colonel Clay Wood, staff officer of General Howard
7. Answers will vary but could include: to add credibility to the information being presented.
8. Answers will vary but could include: the Nez Percé had always been peace-loving people and allies of the United States government; the government did not negotiate with the legitimate Nez Percé chiefs; the government did not live up to its obligations under the treaties it signed (the payments were not paid); the land belonged to the Nez Percé
9. Troops had assembled to drive him from his homeland.
10. The decision reversed his earlier order and allowed non-Nez Percé to move into the Wallowa Valley to settle.

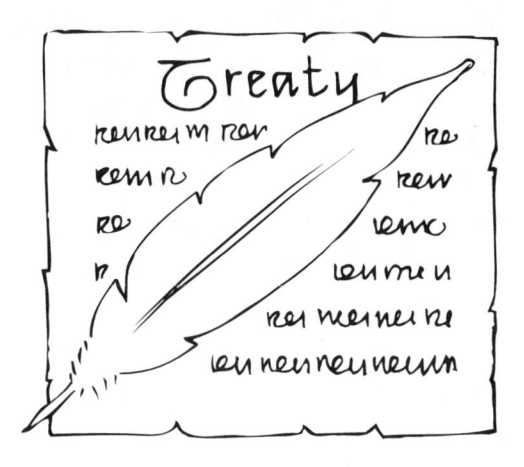

"Every Dog" (No Distinction Of Color) "Has His Day," page 40

1. A Native American
2. A Chinese immigrant
3. A recently freed slave
4. After the Civil War and the passage of the 14th and 15th Amendments, African Americans were hoping to gain equal rights in the United States.
5. The poster above the heads of the two men, show the movement of settlers west, which crowded out Native Americans. The Chinese, it was feared, would migrate west and crowd out settlers from Europe.
6. The poster shows how much the railroad played in the migration of settlers to the west. It also shows the importance of the railroad in bringing Chinese to America. Chinese were imported to America as cheap laborers to work on the railroad construction. As the railroad moved east from California, so did the Chinese workers.
7. It is clear that the poster at the feet of the two men talking is directed at the most recent immigrants to the United States at the time—the Irish and the Dutch. The poster also claims the philosophy of the American Know-Nothing Party.

47

Answer Key

8. According to the cartoon, Chinese are being discriminated against because they are coming to America in big numbers and are threatening to crowd out people already here.
9. The cartoon clearly implies that there is discrimination against Native Americans, Chinese, Irish, Dutch and African Americans. The posters on the walls speak out against the Chinese, the Irish and the Dutch. The two men in the cartoon acknowledge the discrimination against Native Americans. And the African American in the background, is still waiting for equality, demonstrating that there is none yet.
10. The cartoonist is in favor of extending rights to immigrants. He uses satire to show how intolerable discrimination is.

"Move On!" Editorial Cartoon Questions, page 42

1. voting
2. The sign above the men reads, "The Polls."
3. It looks corrupt.
4. The men look like they may be Irish. The man holding a fist full of ballots has a shamrock in his hat, and he is smoking a traditional Irish pipe. Another man has a pipe in his pocket. Some of the other men are wearing traditional Irish clothes.
5. voting
6. The Native American has feathers, long braids and is wearing moccasins. Over his shoulder, in the background is a Native American village with teepees.
7. The cartoonist uses satire here by showing that voting is corrupt and not civilized, though, it is thought to be too civilized for the Native American, who is considered to be uncivilized.
8. That it is also satirical that people born in this country are not allowed to vote, while those who immigrate to America can.
9. A naturalized citizen is one who becomes a citizen by virtue of taking a test and a pledge.
10. Yes, answers will vary.